DESIGN CHALLENGE:

Northwind Quilts

BY SHARYN SQUIER CRAIG

CHITRA PUBLICATIONS

Your best value in quilting!

Chitra Publications
2 Public Avenue
Montrose, Pennsylvania 18801

Second Printing: 1997

Library of Congress Cataloging-in-Publication Data

Craig, Sharyn Squier, 1947-
    Design challenge : northwind quilts / by Sharyn Squier Craig.
        p. cm.
    ISBN 1-885588-17-8
    1. Patchwork.   2. Patchwork--Patterns.   3. Quilting.   4. Quilting--
--Patterns.   I. Title
TT835.C724 1997
746.46'041--dc21   97-17299
                                                                        CIP

Editors: Nancy Roberts and Joyce Libal
Design and Illustrations: Kimberly L. Grace
Cover Photography: Guy Cali Associates, Inc., Clarks Summit, PA
Inside Photography: Ken Jacques Photography, San Diego, CA,
Van Zandbergen Photography, Brackney, PA
Craiges Photography, Montrose, PA
The hoop on the front cover was graciously supplied by:
Norwood Frames
P.O. Box 167 • Fremont, MI • 49417
Phone: (616) 924-3901

The quilt rack on the front cover was graciously supplied by:
Hinterburg Design, Inc.
2805 East Progress Drive • West Bend, WI 53095
Phone: (414) 338-0337

Our Mission Statement

*We publish quality quilting magazines and books
that recognize, promote and inspire self-expression.
We are dedicated to serving our customers
with respect, kindness and efficiency.*

I have always loved traditional quilt blocks and am especially drawn to directional ones such as the Northwind block. That's because the design potential with such blocks is so exciting, as you'll see in this book.

Perhaps you recognize "Creativity in Motion," the quilt (page 10) that inspired this Design Challenge. It's the Northwind quilt that was shown on the cover of my first book, Designing New Traditions in Quilts *(Chitra Publications, 1991). I first ran into the block in an old quilt calendar from E.P. Dutton. The block was used in a quilt called Ocean Waves. I could imagine this block creating the look of an Ocean Waves design as you can see in the quilt shown here and on page 9. But I could also imagine simply turning the blocks and coloring them differently for brand new looks.*

Once Designing New Traditions in Quilts *hit the market, the interest generated by the cover quilt truly amazed me. In response, I continued exploring the use of the block. This resulted in the Northwind Design Challenge, published in Issue 38 of* Traditional Quiltworks.

I've been teaching Northwind workshops since 1993 and continue to be impressed with the new designs you quilters dream up. It's one of those quilt blocks that seems to have no limits! The desire to share more Northwind design ideas along with the easy sewing system for creating the blocks motivated me to write this book. You'll see a few familiar favorites from that first Design Challenge, but you'll also see lots more incredible quilts to tempt and inspire you. There are more block sizes to choose from, too. So familiarize yourself with the basics, then head for your sewing room and start piecing!

CONTENTS

CHAPTER 1

GETTING STARTED

You'll find that Northwind blocks make fantastic scrap quilts. The method for creating the parts you'll sew together to complete the blocks is perfect for using small pieces of fabric. And the best part of working with scraps is that you can't run out of fabric! Anytime you work with a limited number of fabrics, you have to be careful to buy enough to complete your quilt.

Making scrap quilts doesn't mean you should ignore color. They often have color formulas or "recipes." You can work with limited colors, yet still make a scrappy quilt. Two examples of scrappy quilts made using color formulas are my red and white Northwind quilt on the front cover and on page 13 and my red, white and blue one shown on the front cover and page 9.

Study the block and you'll notice that it is made from two large triangles (cut using Template A found on page 15), three pieced squares and four small triangles (both cut using Template B). You'll begin with a pair of large fabric triangles—one light and one dark. Parts for a Northwind block are rotary cut from the pair, using the two templates.

SUPPLY LIST

- Assorted print fabrics in dark and light values
- Rotary cutter, ruler and mat
- Transparent template plastic, heavyweight fine-grit sandpaper and permanent glue stick or the John Flynn Cut-Your-Own Template Kit™ (see page 15 for ordering information or ask for it at your local quilt shop)
- Sewing Machine

MAKING THE TEMPLATES

You'll find the pattern pieces for three block sizes at the back of this book. Choose a block size, find the corresponding A and B pattern pieces and make a template for each one. If you are using template plastic, follow these steps to make a sturdy template "sandwich":
- Trace the full-size pattern piece on plain white paper.
- Cover the traced pattern piece with glue and place the template plastic on top of it.
- Cover the back of the traced pattern piece with glue and place the back (non-gritty side) of the sandpaper on it.
- Allow all three layers to dry completely and then cut the tem-plate sandwich out with scissors.

CUTTING THE LARGE TRIANGLES

Northwind Block Chart

Block Size	Fabric Triangles (short sides measure)
4 1/2"	7 1/2"
6"	9"
7 1/2"	10 1/2"

- Check the Northwind Block Chart under Fabric Triangles to determine the correct side measurement for your block size.
- Place a light and a dark fabric right sides together and cut fabric triangles with a side measurement equal to that listed in the chart. If you don't mind repeating fabrics in the quilt, you may prefer to cut squares this size and then cut them in half to yield two pairs of triangles. One light + one dark triangle = one pair. Each pair will make one Northwind block.
- Continue cutting pairs of triangles for as many blocks as you wish to make. I suggest starting your design play with 36 blocks.

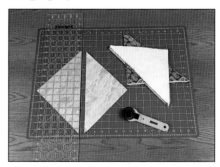

- Matching the longest edges of the triangles, stack the pairs in sets of four. Then stack the sets, alternating the direction of the triangles.

CHAPTER 2

MAKING PARTS FOR NORTHWIND BLOCKS

I've developed a quick method for creating parts for Northwind blocks. You'll slice sets of triangles into two pieces. After sewing pairs of "etceteras" as described below, you'll rotary cut the block pieces using the templates. To determine the correct cutting measurement, check the Etcetera Cutting Chart on page 6 for the block size you are making. Then follow these steps:

REMINDER:

1 pair = 1 light & 1 dark triangle
1 set = 4 pair (that's 4 light & 4 dark triangles)

• Position one set of triangles (4 pair) on the mat so the square corner of the set points toward your hand that's holding the rotary cutter. Using a rotary cutting ruler, measure from the long diagonal edge and slice through all 8 layers. You'll create smaller triangles and "etceteras"—my term for the odd-shaped pieces. Cut all of the sets this way.

• Position the A template on one set of triangles and cut around it. You'll be cutting through 8 layers.

• Take one pair of "etceteras" and sew them along their long edge. Continue chain sewing the remaining pairs. Clip the units apart.

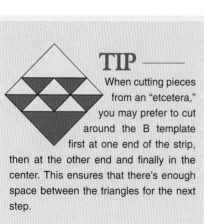

TIP

When cutting pieces from an "etcetera," you may prefer to cut around the B template first at one end of the strip, then at the other end and finally in the center. This ensures that there's enough space between the triangles for the next step.

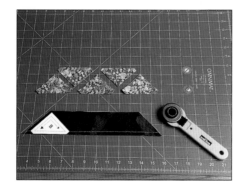

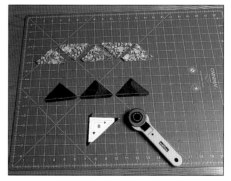

• Position the B template on the sewn edge of a pieced "etcetera," as shown aligning the points on the blunted ends of the template with the sewn line. Cut around the template.

• Move the template, position it as before and cut again, leaving about 1/2" between triangles. Repeat to cut a third B from the pieced "etcetera."

• Stack the two leftover areas from the "etceteras." Position the B template on the stack and cut around it.

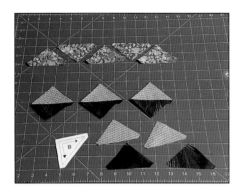

Etcetera Cutting Chart		
Block Size	Fabric Triangles	Measure from long side and slice at:
4 1/2"	7 1/2"	2"
6"	9"	2 1/4"
7 1/2"	10 1/2"	2 3/4"

Cutting this way results in three pieced squares and four unattached triangles from each pieced "etcetera."

• Open the pieced squares and finger press the seam allowances toward the darker fabric.

• Repeat the steps to cut A's and B's from all of the triangle sets.

Now you're ready to assemble the blocks using the sewing system in the next chapter.

CHAPTER 3

SEWING BLOCKS WITH A SYSTEM

Take the parts for one block—two large triangles (one light, one dark), three pieced squares and four small triangles. Lay out the parts for the center section of the block, as shown. The numbers indicate the order in which you'll sew the seams. Set the large triangles (A's) aside for now and follow the steps to piece the center section.

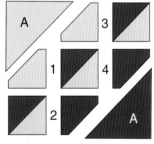

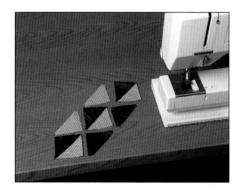

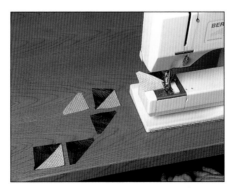

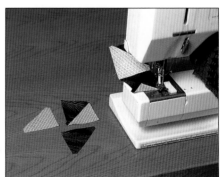

To sew the center section:

• Pick up the two units indicated by #1. Place the pieced square at the right on the triangle at the left, right sides together, and sew them along the right edge.

• At the end of the seam, leave the presser foot down and the unit in your machine.

• Pick up the units for seam 2, placing the triangle at the right on the pieced square at the left. Sew them along the right edge and stop, as before.

- Sew seam 3 in the same manner, placing the pieced square on the triangle, and stop.
- Leaving the thread connecting the first two units intact, clip the threads joining them to unit three. This frees the first two units while the third one remains in the sewing machine.

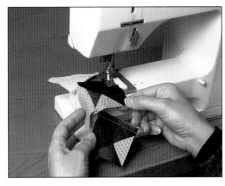

- Bring the first two units to the front of the presser foot. Open up the first unit and finger press the seam allowance toward the single triangle. Position the remaining triangle on the first unit, right sides together, and sew seam 4.

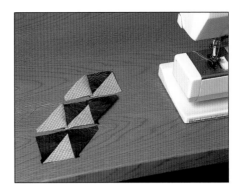

- Clip threads to remove the unit from the machine, but leave all other connecting threads intact. Finger press all seam allowances toward the single triangles. Think of the block center as sewn vertically. Now you must complete the horizontal seams. The connecting threads will ensure that the horizontal seams are sewn correctly.

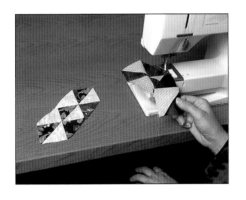

- Place the top two rows right sides together and sew. The seam allowances will face in alternate directions because of the way you pressed them, allowing the seamlines to match perfectly. Repeat to join the second to the third row.

To complete the block:
- Stitch the large A triangles to opposite sides of the center section. Press the seam allowance toward the A triangles.

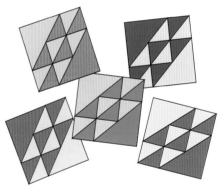

- Use the same sewing sequence to make as many blocks as you have made parts for. I call each block with this light and dark value placement Block A. Now you're ready to use the blocks for some design fun.

CHAPTER 4

DESIGN WALL PLAY

Now the design enjoyment begins! A design wall is a must for creating your quilt. I use a flannel sheet secured to the wall with thumbtacks. If you don't have wall space available, use a door. Another possibility is tacking the flannel to wooden stretcher bars and leaning it against the wall when you're ready to design. The blocks will adhere to the flannel, which allows you to arrange them any way you like.

You'll find that directional blocks such as the Northwind are versatile. Using them in traditional-style Log Cabin arrangements is my favorite approach. Think Barn Raising, Fields and Furrows or Streak of Lightning, and place your blocks in these layouts just as if they were Log Cabin blocks. My quilt shown in Chapter 5 (page 14) is made using a Field and Furrows setting.

If your scrappy blocks look too busy when you get them on the design wall, try grouping blocks with like colors together. That's what I did in "Creativity in Motion" (page 10). The result was definitely more pleasing to my eye. You might also add sashing strips to provide a resting place for the eye as Margret Reap did in her quilt (below).

The thing to remember while designing is to work quickly. Put your blocks up, take them down and rearrange them. This way, design ideas will flow. Ready, set… play!

◀

I selected 32 Block A's in colors suitable for a baby quilt and set them on point in this quilt. Placing the blocks randomly created a lively collage of triangles which are framed with pink print setting triangles.

▶

See what a difference sashing makes! Margret Reap set four Block A's together with light strips and a contrasting cornerstone. Then she used dark strips to set the four-block units together for a wonderful windowpane effect. This rich, masculine-looking quilt resulted.

▶

To capture an old-time feel in this quilt, I used Harriet Hargrave's line of red, white and blue reproduction prints manufactured by P&B Textiles. All of the block parts were made using the methods in Chapter 2, but notice how I mixed them up when sewing the blocks. The blocks are set together Pinwheel-style, giving the quilt the look of the Ocean Waves design.

▼

Mary Pavlovich concentrated on dark blues and rosy pinks in her color palette, creating a quilt with a non-traditional feel. Notice the band of light through the quilt center and how some of the blocks pierce the border.

▼

Barbara Hutchins used a border stripe for some of the large triangles in her quilt which resulted in a fascinating design.

◀

"Creativity in Motion" appeared on the cover of my first book, Designing New Traditions in Quilts. When I first arranged the Block A's on the flannel wall, they appeared too busy. Grouping the blocks by color on the design wall calmed the design and made it more pleasing.

CHAPTER 5

AMAZING NORTHWIND VARIATIONS

There's more in store for you with this block! It's time to ask "What If…?" What if you color the block differently? What fun to use the same parts and just turn them to come up with brand new looks. Everything stays the same—pairing the triangles, making the parts, the sewing system—except the way the block and the finished quilt looks. You'll be amazed.

Here are seven more block design variations to play with. Remember, the original block is called Block A. Make these simple changes to make Blocks B to H, comparing each one to the original Block A. But don't stop there! Perhaps you'll come up with yet another arrangement.

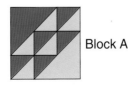

Block A

• To make Block B, you need only switch the positions of the large light and dark triangles.

Block B

• To make Block C, just turn the two pieced squares at the corners to reverse the placement of the small dark and light triangles.

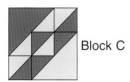

Block C

• Block D is like Block C, but the positions of the large triangles are reversed.

Block D

• For Block E, start with Block B and turn the pieced squares in the corners of the block so the small light triangles point out.

Block E

▶
Homespun fabrics and Block B's take on a fresh, country look in Carolyn Smith's quilt.

• Block F is similar to Block E, but the positions of the large light and dark triangles are reversed.

Block F

• Lay out Block G like Block E, but turn the pieced squares in the corners so that the small dark triangles point out.

Block G

• Lay out Block H the same as Block G, but reverse the positions of the large light and dark triangles.

Block H

You might think that such small alterations won't effect how quilts made with these new blocks look. But the quilts shown here demonstrate some of the dramatic designs you can get with simple changes. I'll bet you could play with Northwind blocks for years and never make the same quilt twice!

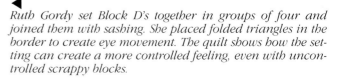

◀
Ruth Gordy set Block D's together in groups of four and joined them with sashing. She placed folded triangles in the border to create eye movement. The quilt shows how the setting can create a more controlled feeling, even with uncontrolled scrappy blocks.

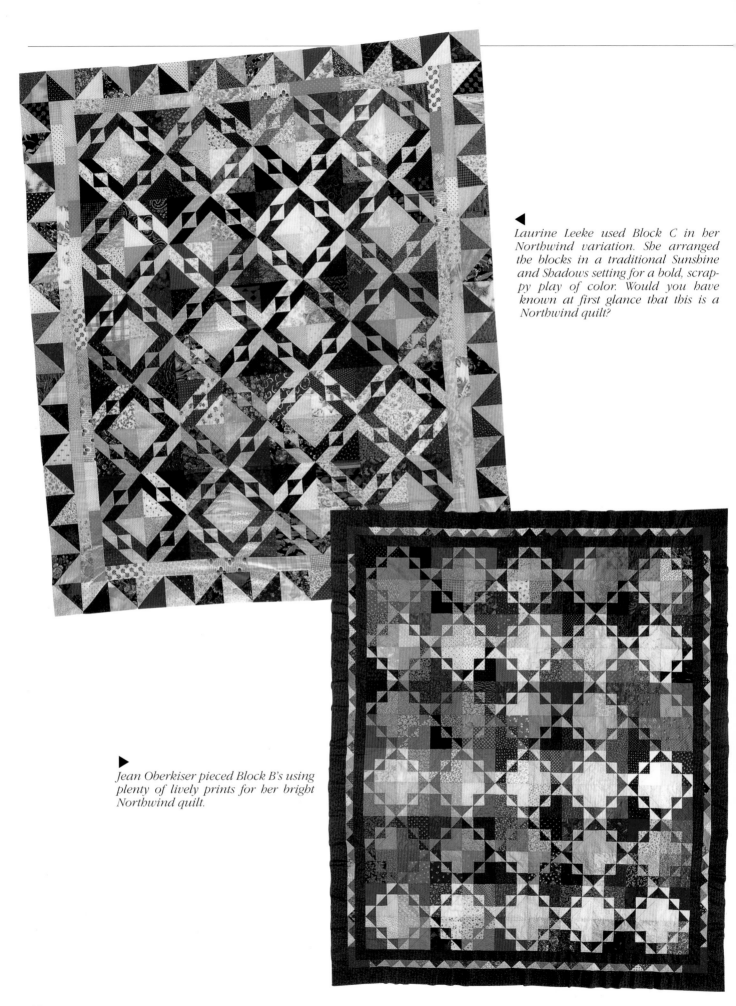

◄ Laurine Leeke used Block C in her Northwind variation. She arranged the blocks in a traditional Sunshine and Shadows setting for a bold, scrappy play of color. Would you have known at first glance that this is a Northwind quilt?

► Jean Oberkiser pieced Block B's using plenty of lively prints for her bright Northwind quilt.

▶ *Dozens of fabrics enliven this quilt made using G and H blocks. It has a medallion-like look. The outside border is composed of block parts.*

◀ *What if you used only one light fabric with many dark prints of one color? That's what I did in this quilt made with Block B's. I also combined different reds in every block rather than using one red print for each.*

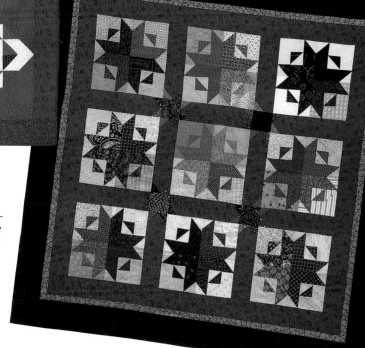

▶ *An impressive Northwind Star emerged when Linda Packer set four Block E's together. She repeated the design element by creating small pieced stars in the sashing.*

I used a traditional Fields and Furrows set in this Northwind quilt made using B blocks.

Dark prints spiced with some jewel tones create a deep, rich look in Sandy Andersen's quilt made with Block B's. She began with one light fabric and many dark ones, but added a few more lights when she used all of the original one. That's the beauty of scrap quilts—you never run out of fabric!

Full-Size Pattern Pieces for the Northwind Block

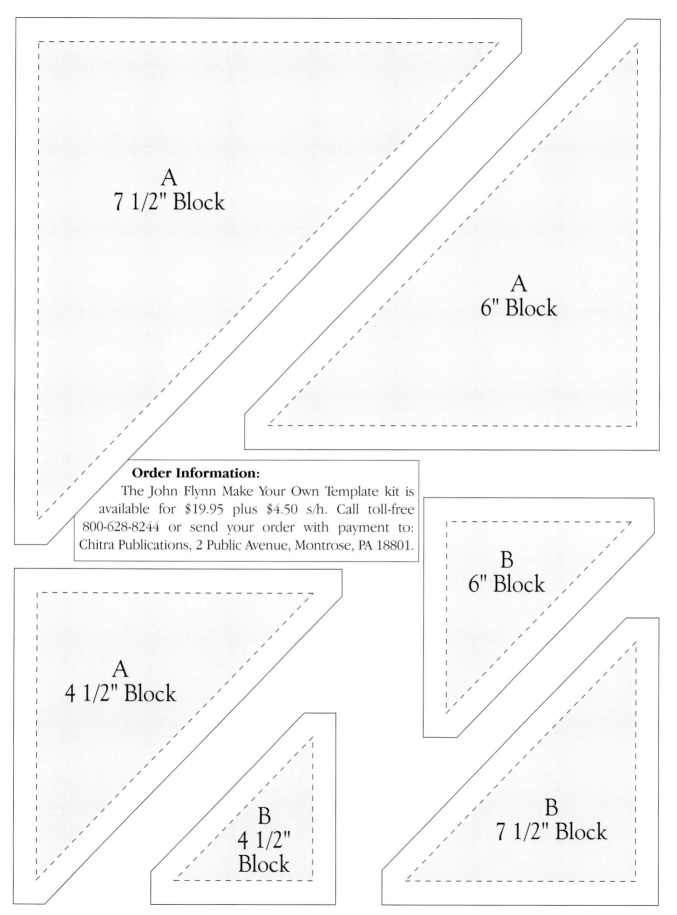

A
7 1/2" Block

A
6" Block

Order Information:
The John Flynn Make Your Own Template kit is available for $19.95 plus $4.50 s/h. Call toll-free 800-628-8244 or send your order with payment to: Chitra Publications, 2 Public Avenue, Montrose, PA 18801.

B
6" Block

A
4 1/2" Block

B
4 1/2"
Block

B
7 1/2" Block

Coloring Diagrams
for the Northwind Block

To experiment with color, make several photocopies of this page,
take your crayons or markers in hand and start coloring!